Great Storytellers

The Mythical World of Rick Riordan

Anita Yasuda

LIGHTBOX
openlightbox.com

LIGHTBOX

Go to
www.openlightbox.com
and enter this book's unique code.

ACCESS CODE

LBM36382

Lightbox is an all-inclusive digital solution for the teaching and learning of curriculum topics in an original, groundbreaking way. Lightbox is based on National Curriculum Standards.

STANDARD FEATURES OF LIGHTBOX

AUDIO High-quality narration using text-to-speech system

ACTIVITIES Printable PDFs that can be emailed and graded

SLIDESHOWS Pictorial overviews of key concepts

VIDEOS Embedded high-definition video clips

WEBLINKS Curated links to external, child-safe resources

TRANSPARENCIES Step-by-step layering of maps, diagrams, charts, and timelines

INTERACTIVE MAPS Interactive maps and aerial satellite imagery

QUIZZES Ten multiple choice questions that are automatically graded and emailed for teacher assessment

KEY WORDS Matching key concepts to their definitions

Contents

Rick launched his book *The Lost Heroes* with a big event in Austin, Texas.

Introducing Rick Riordan

Rick Riordan has passed on his love of ***mythology*** *to a whole generation of young readers around the world. What began as a bedtime story for his sons launched his career as a hugely successful author of books for children and young adults.*

Costumes and props add to the excitement of Rick's book launches.

What story made Rick Riordan famous?

Rick Riordan's two most popular children's series are Percy Jackson & the Olympians and The Kane Chronicles. These books have earned him fans all over the world.

What is so special about Rick's books?

Ever since he was young, Rick was interested in myths, especially the mythology of ancient Greece. Myths often have characters that have supernatural powers. They throw thunderbolts and cause storms to occur. Rick was attracted to the drama and fantasy of these stories. Rick liked to tell myths as bedtime stories to his own children. However, he eventually ran out of myths to tell. When this happened, he began creating his own stories based on mythical characters. These stories later became published books.

"I can't remember a time when I wasn't interested in mythology..."

How has Rick contributed to education?

Today, Rick's books entertain children of all ages. At the same time, they teach children about the history and myths of ancient **civilizations**. As a former teacher, Rick's greatest reward is hearing about kids who have become readers because of his books.

Once Upon a Time

Rick Riordan was born on June 5, 1964. He grew up in San Antonio, Texas. His parents were very young when they got married and started a family. Rick's parents and grandparents were all teachers. His father, Rick Riordan, Sr., was a **vocational** teacher. Rick's mother, Lyn Belisle, taught English, art, and **graphic design**. She was a writer, artist and musician, as well.

"Having parents who read is critical, because modeling that behavior will show children that reading is an important and enjoyable part of family life."

Rick grew up in a loving and creative home. It was a gathering place for artists, actors, and authors. Rick's mother allowed Rick to discover his own interests. Whenever Rick complained of being bored, his mother encouraged him to think of different activities he might enjoy doing. She wanted Rick to find ways to entertain himself. This gave Rick the opportunity to daydream and develop his imagination.

San Antonio is the second most populated city in Texas with a population of 1.4 million.

Rick's father was also artistic. He liked to write poetry and make pottery. He often took Rick along with him to his pottery class. Rick would make dinosaur sculptures while his father worked on his pottery. They would then try to sell their creations at the market.

At night, Rick's father would read bedtime stories to his son. He was a storyteller who instilled in Rick a love of reading. Many of Rick's favorite stories came from a book called *Tales of the Western World*. Rick enjoyed the Native American myths and American **folktales** from the book. Another favorite book was *Fletcher and Zenobia* by Edward Gorey. Rick also enjoyed the dark humor of Roald Dahl's books.

All 5 Percy Jackson and the Olympians books were in *USA Today*'s Top 10 Best Sellers at the same time.

The Red Pyramid sold more than 90,000 copies in the first week.

The first two Percy Jackson films made nearly $430 million.

Roald Dahl's book *James and the Giant Peach* was one of Rick's favourite books when he was a boy.

One of the first books that Rick read for fun was J.R.R. Tolkein's *The Fellowship of the Ring.*

School Years

Rick was a quiet child. He liked to spend his time building toys he could play with. Rick could often be found playing with Lego or putting a toy robot together. Rick also liked going to school. He often thought that he could explain the lesson just as well as the teacher did.

Rick was not a keen reader as a child, however. He enjoyed the stories his parents read to him at home, but did not like the books he had to read at school. Rick could not relate to the stories. It was only when Rick was about 12 years of age that he began to enjoy reading. This was largely thanks to his eighth grade English teacher. Mrs. Pabst became aware of Rick's dislike of the school's reading list. She began to look for books that might appeal to the reluctant reader.

"...I often asked teachers what I should write about, only to be given that old axiom, 'Write about what you know.'"

Books such as J.R.R. Tolkien's series The Lord of The Rings captivated young Rick. Mrs. Pabst told Rick that the Tolkien books were inspired by **Norse** mythology. Rick started studying books on this topic. As he learned more about the fantasy **genre**, Rick became interested in creating stories similar to those he was reading.

Rick began writing short stories, and even tried to have his work published. Rick was only 12 years old when he sent his first short story to *Isaac Asimov's Science Fiction Magazine*. Isaac Asimov was an award-winning science fiction author. Even though the story was not accepted for publication, Rick enjoyed the writing process. He continued to write and won a prize in a university writing contest.

Map of Texas

OKLAHOMA
Santa Fe
Oklahoma City
ARKANSAS
Little Rock
NEW MEXICO
Forth Worth
Dallas
El Paso
TEXAS
Austin
LOUISIANA
Baton Rouge
Houston
San Antonio
Gulf of Mexico
MEXICO
Capital
City
Border
Water
Texas
Land
0
250 Kilometers
250 Miles
N

Early Writing

Although Rick enjoyed writing, he also developed an interest in music. After high school, Rick thought that he wanted to become a musician. He enjoyed playing the guitar and had dreams of becoming a rock star. Rick decided to attend North Texas State to study music. This university is now called University of North Texas. It has one of the largest collections of music in the United States.

"A good book always keeps you asking questions, and makes you keep turning pages..."

Despite his interest in music, Rick's English classes made him realize how important **literature** was to him. He discovered books that he had never read in high school. He began to think about becoming an English teacher. He liked the idea of being able to read and discuss books for a living.

Rick decided to transfer to the University of Texas at Austin. Here, he began working towards a degree in English and history.

University of Texas at Austin is one of the biggest universities in the United States.

Rick also continued to develop his own writing. He was able to get two of his short stories published in the university's literary magazine.

Rick graduated from university in 1986. Two years later, he received his teaching certificate. He also married. He and his wife Becky then moved to San Francisco, California. There, Rick began studying for a degree in English and **Medieval** Studies. He later accepted a teaching position at a local school. For the next few years, Rick taught English and history to middle school students. All the while, he continued to write. He decided to focus his attention on writing mysteries.

More than 40 million copies of Rick's books are in print in the U.S.

Rick has won all three of the top mystery book awards in the U.S.

Rick's books have been translated into more than 37 languages.

Rick taught English at Presidio Hill School in San Francisco for eight years.

Road to Success

Rick enjoyed teaching in the San Francisco Bay area. He loved getting to know his students and seeing them mature. He also enjoyed teaching them about literature, especially mythology. Rick worked hard as a teacher. He wanted his students to be excited about learning. He wanted them to leave his room wanting to read more, not less.

> "It just felt different than anything else I'd ever written, because the novel had practically forced me to write it."

Rick was teaching all day and going to school himself. Yet, he still found time to write short stories. He often submitted them to magazine publishers to see if they would publish them. He was rewarded in 1998. The *Mary Higgins Clark Mystery Magazine* published his short story 'A Small Silver Gun.' Some of Rick's other stories were then published in *Ellery Queen's Mystery Magazine*. This is the oldest and longest running short-story mystery magazine in the world.

Rick liked living in San Francisco, but there were times when he missed San Antonio. In order to feel closer to home, he decided to write a book based in his hometown. *Big Red Tequila* follows a private detective called Tres Navarre as he tries to solve a mystery in San Antonio.

Bantam Books published Big Red Tequila in 1997. The book won several literary awards, such as the Anthony Award for best original paperback. It also got the Shamus award for best first private investigator novel. A year later, Rick released the **sequel**. With *The Widower's Two-Step*, Rick was on his way to becoming a successful author.

After Rick and Becky's children were born, Rick and his family moved back to San Antonio. Rick taught at a private school, Saint Mary's Hall. In 2002, Saint Mary's Hall honored him with the school's first Master Teacher Award. Rick continued teaching while writing in his spare time for another six years.

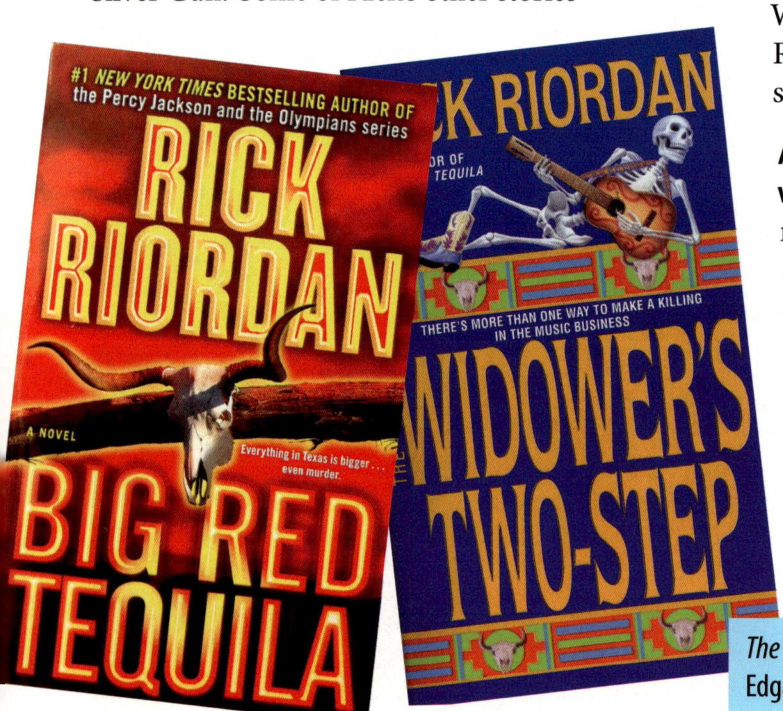

The Widower's Two-Step won the 1998 Edgar Award for Best Paperback Original.

Tres Navarre from *Big Red Tequila* grew up in Bexar County, San Antonio.

Creative Writing Tips

Writing a story or a poem can be challenging, but it can also be very rewarding. Some writers have trouble coming up with ideas. Others have so many ideas that they do not know where to start. Rick Riordan has special writing habits that young writers can follow to develop their own ideas and stories.

Tip 1 Find Inspiration

Good writers are excited about their subjects. Think about what excites or interests you. It could be a person or an activity. It could even be a dream you have had. Rick was inspired by his own interest in mythology to create new mythological characters and exciting adventures.

Tip 2 Write, Write, Write

Sometimes, it is a good idea to write as much as possible in a first **draft**. Very few writers have ever produced a great story in just one draft. Instead, they review their first draft to see which parts to keep and what needs to be **revised**. When Rick first started writing stories, he showed his work to his students. They gave him feedback and helped him decide which parts of the story worked well and which parts needed to be changed.

Tip 3

The Creative Process

Most writers have different opinions about when is the best time to write. Some work best late at night when everyone else is asleep. Others claim that they are most productive early in the morning. Rick does not have a set writing schedule. Usually, he writes early in the morning or late at night when the house is quiet. Often, his writing time is scheduled in between family activities and business.

Tip 4

It Takes Dedication

Writing takes dedication and **discipline**. Rick worked for 15 years as a teacher and wrote stories in his spare time. It took months for him to finish a book. Rick advises aspiring writers to keep writing their stories, even if they feel they need more time to write the story properly. He believes that people who really want to write will always find the time. Rick also encourages writers to never give up. They need to keep trying until they find the story that they were truly meant to tell.

Fantastic Fiction

Although he has written books for adults, Rick Riordan enjoys writing for children. He is best known for his novels for young adults. His fantasy adventure books, including the Percy Jackson & the Olympians series, appeal to readers of all ages.

The Lightning Thief

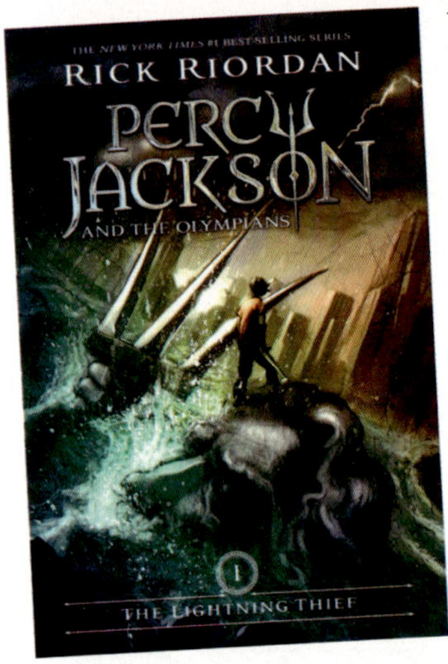

Rick Riordan's first book tells the story of 12-year-old Percy Jackson. Percy discovers he is half human and half god after accidentally vaporising his math teacher. Percy's father is Poseidon, god of the sea. Percy is sent to Camp Half-Blood. There he meets other children who are the offspring of a human and a god. He makes some new friends, Grover and Annabeth. While at the camp, Percy discovers that the thunderbolt of Zeus has been stolen. Percy and his friends set out on a quest to recover the missing thunderbolt.

AWARDS

2005 New York Times Notable Book

2006 Red House Children's Book Award

The Sea of Monsters

AWARDS

2006 Book Sense Top Ten Summer Pick

The Sea of Monsters is the second book in the Percy Jackson series. Percy and his friends must find the **Golden Fleece** in order to save Camp Half-Blood from monsters. During his quest, Percy has many exciting adventures. He sails into the dreaded Sea of Monsters. He rescues his friend Grover from the Cyclops's island. He even saves Annabeth from drowning. Percy also discovers a disturbing family secret. It makes him wonder if being the son of Poseidon is something to be proud of after all.

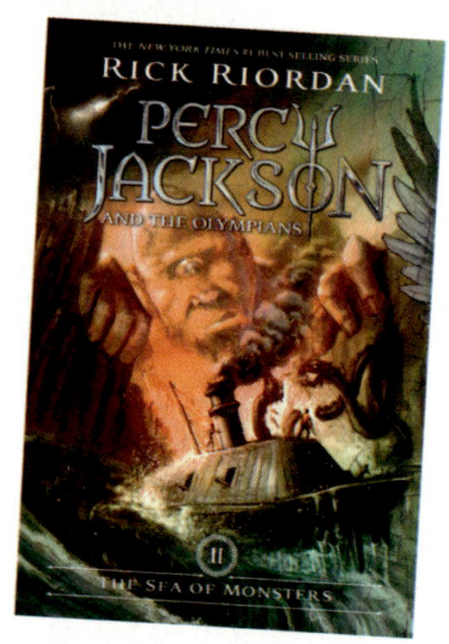

The Maze of Bones

Several top authors collaborated on the 39 Clues series. Rick wrote the first book in the series, *The Maze of Bones.* It is about the adventures of Dan and Amy Cahill. When Dan and Amy's grandmother dies, her will reveals a family secret. Dan and Amy learn that they are part of the most important family in the world. They are given the choice to either receive $1 million or go on a quest to find a priceless treasure. Dan and Amy decide to go on the quest. Their travels take them all the way to Paris, France. There, they compete with others searching for the clues to an ancient mystery.

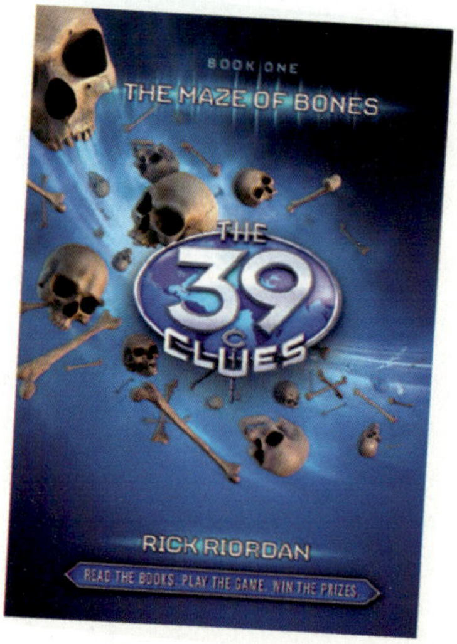

The Lost Hero

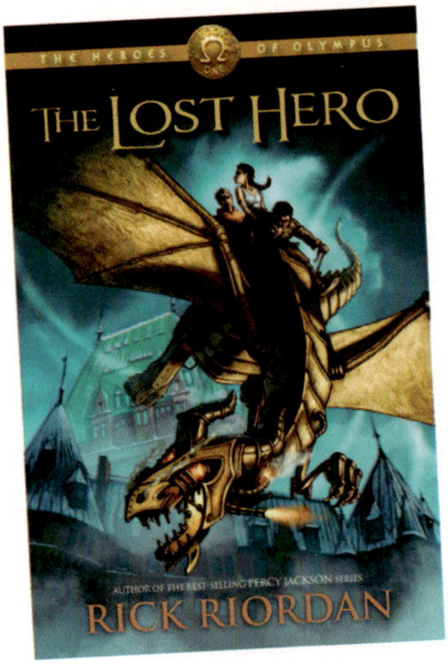

The Lost Hero is a book about the importance of friendship. It is part of Rick's Heroes of Olympus series. The main character in the series is Jason. When the story begins, Jason is sitting in a school bus. He has no idea who he is or where he is. Fortunately, other people on the bus know him and inform Jason that he is on a field trip to the Grand Canyon. When one of the other students on the bus turns into a storm spirit, Jason is thrust into the world of Greek and Roman gods. Along with his friends Piper and Leo, Jason sets out on a journey to save Hera, queen of the gods.

AWARDS

2010 Barnes and Noble Best Book Award

2013 Junior Young Reader's Choice Award

The Red Pyramid

AWARDS

2010
A School Library Journal Best Book

2011
Children's Choice Best Book

The Red Pyramid is the first book in The Kane Chronicles series. It features siblings Carter and Sadie Kane. Since their mother's death, Sadie has lived with her grandparents in London. Carter has been traveling the world with their father. He is a scientist who studies ancient Egypt. He takes the children to the British Museum, where he summons Set, an ancient Egyptian god. In the exciting adventure that ensues, Carter and Sadie end up struggling to save their father. As they do so, they learn that they are descended from the most powerful magicians in ancient Egypt.

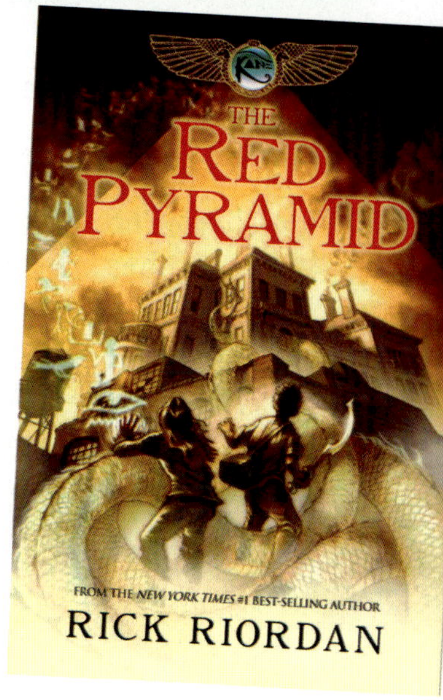

The Son of Neptune

The Son of Neptune is the second book in the Heroes of Olympus series. When Percy Jackson awakens from a long sleep, he finds that he has lost his memory. He can only remember his own name and that of his friend, Annabeth. Percy ends up on a mission for Mars, the leader of the Roman camp. Percy must travel to Alaska with his new friends on a dangerous quest. They must rescue Thanatos, the god of death. The friends must overcome many perils to achieve their mission. Percy and his friends must also fight a terrifying battle to save the Roman camp from destruction.

AWARDS

2011
Goodreads Choice Awards

Vespers Rising

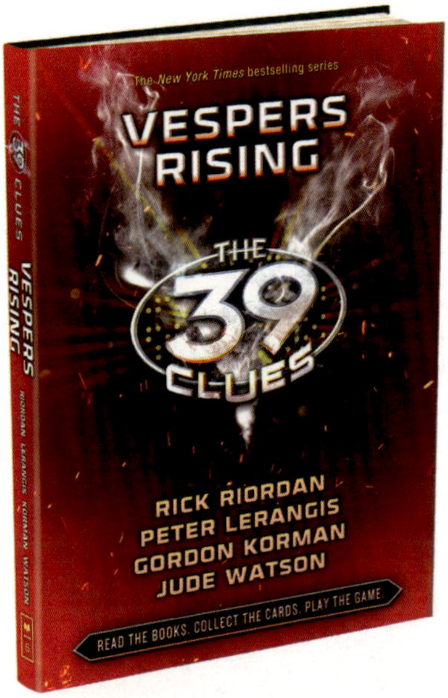

This action-packed book is part of The 39 Clues series. Rick Riordan, Gordon Korman, Peter Lerangis, and Jude Watson wrote the book together. Each author created his own story within the book. The reader is taken on a journey back in time to the year 1507. The origins of the Cahill family secret are revealed. Rick's story is about Gideon Cahill, the patriarch of the Cahill family. In this book, the reader finds out about the dramatic events that tore Gideon's family apart. The novel also explains the origin of the 39 clues that are the main theme of the series.

The Sword of Summer

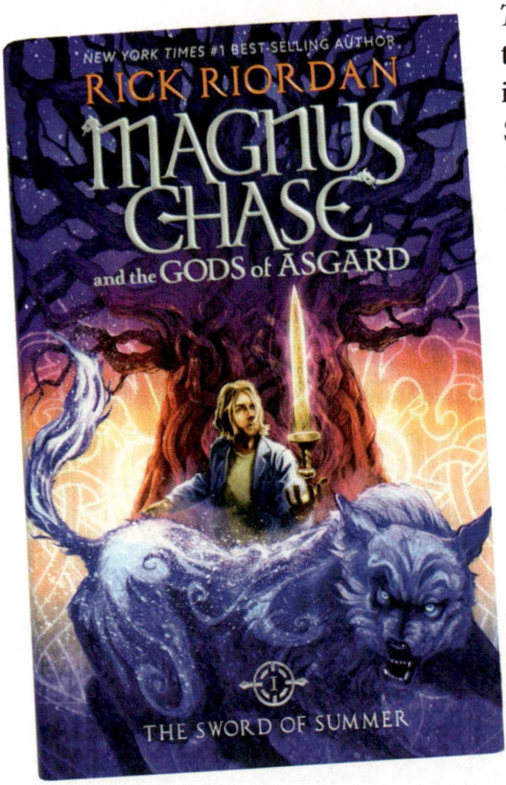

The Sword of Summer is the first of three books in the Magnus Chase Series. Magnus Chase is a 16-year-old living on the streets when an astonishing secret is revealed to him. He is the son of a Norse god! No sooner does he begin to digest this news, than he is pulled into the terrifying world of trolls, giants, and Viking gods. Magnus must make some courageous decisions as he tries to save innocent lives from untold dangers.

AWARDS

2015 Goodreads Choice Awards

Milestones

1964

Rick Riordan is born in San Antonio, Texas, on June 5.

1988

Rick receives his teaching certificate. Soon after, he and his wife move to San Francisco, California.

1997

Rick publishes his first novel, an adult mystery called *Big Red Tequila*.

2005

Percy Jackson & the Olympians: The Lightning Thief is published.

2007

Rick's third book for the Percy Jackson series, *The Titan's Curse,* goes to Number 1 on the New York Times best-seller list.

2010

The movie *Percy Jackson & the Olympians: The Lightning Thief* is released.

2013

The movie *Percy Jackson: Sea of Monsters* is released.

2016

The Hidden Oracle, the first book of the Trials of Apollo series, is published.

Breakthrough Books

Rick felt it was important to pass his love of reading on to his two sons, Patrick and Haley. Like his father, Haley loved to listen to bedtime stories. He especially liked Greek myths. One evening, Rick ran out of Greek myths to tell his son. Haley was disappointed and asked his father to create a new myth. In the course of three evenings, Rick created the character of Percy Jackson, who must go on a quest to recover the lightning bolt of Zeus. Haley loved the story. He suggested that Rick write a book about it.

"It's not a bad thing to be different. Sometimes, it's the mark of being very, very talented. That's what Percy discovers about himself in *The Lightning Thief*."

Before long, Rick set to work writing his first children's book. He decided to base the character of Percy Jackson on Haley. Percy and Haley both have **attention deficit hyperactivity disorder** (ADHD) and **dyslexia**. While writing, Rick looked to his boys for guidance. He would read his **manuscript** aloud to his sons. If their interest began to waver, he would rewrite the text until it held their attention right to the end.

***The Lightning Thief* was published in 2005.** It became an instant success. Rick continued the Percy Jackson series with four more books. Each went on to be a best seller. The series has been published in more than 30 countries. Worldwide, it has sold more than 20 million books.

Rick retired from teaching after the Percy Jackson series was published. He no longer had the time to devote his attention to both of his careers. He decided to become a full-time writer.

Haley Riordan sometimes accompanies his father to writing events. He talks about how he helped Rick develop the Percy Jackson books.

The Publishing Process

Publishing companies receive hundreds of manuscripts from authors each year. Only a few manuscripts become books. Publishers must be sure that a manuscript will sell many copies. As a result, publishers reject most of the manuscripts they receive. Once a manuscript has been accepted, it goes through many stages before it is published. Often, authors change their work to follow an editor's suggestions. Once the book is published, some authors receive royalties. This is money based on book sales.

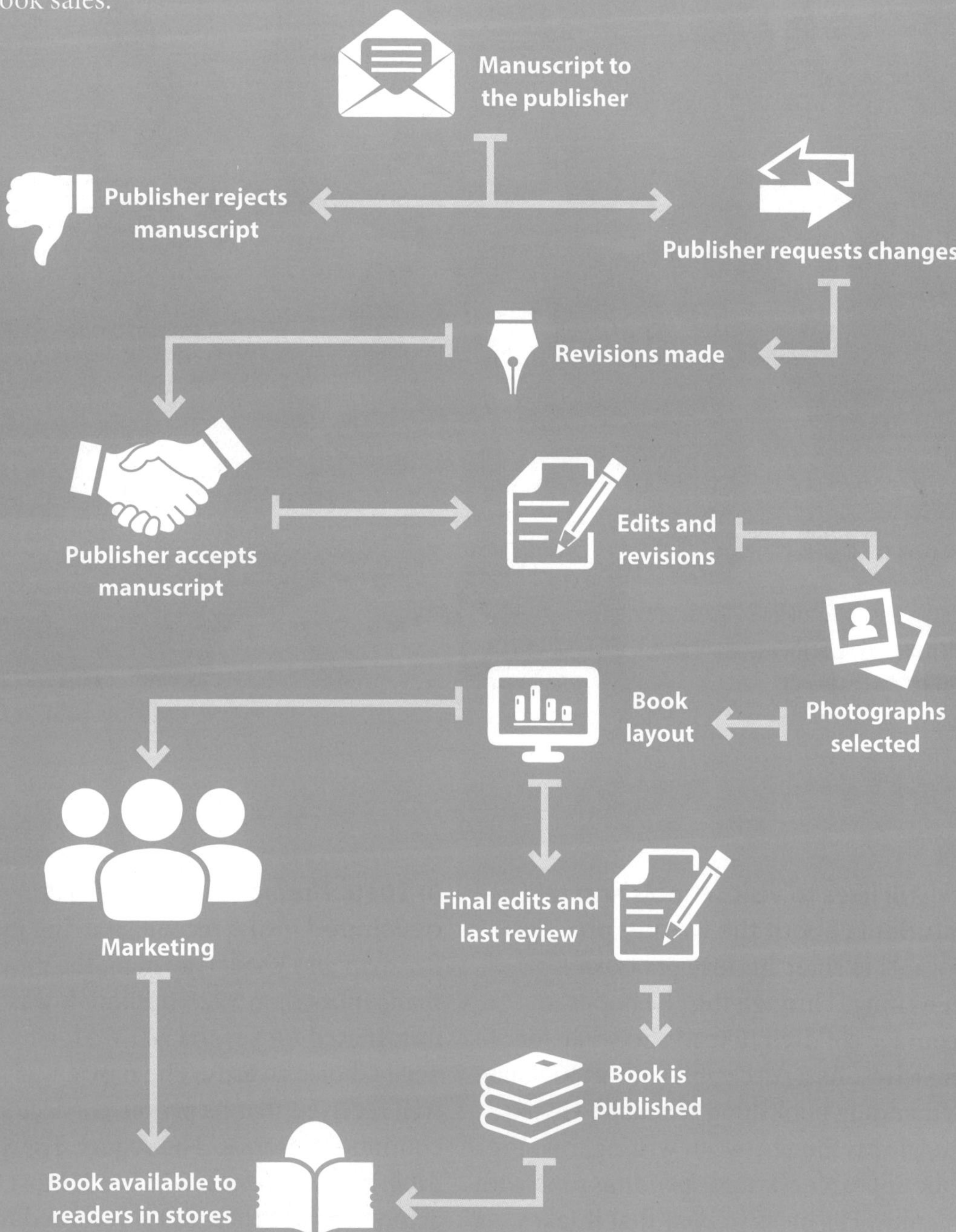

Special events about Rick's books are often attended by thousands of fans.

Latest News

Rick still likes to visit schools and talk to students about the writing process. He wants to share his love of books and writing. Through this, he hopes to encourage children to read and write for themselves. As a successful author, Rick has a demanding publishing schedule. He has to juggle his time between writing, making public appearances, and spending time with his family. His life is so busy that it takes Rick about one year to write each book.

In 2010, *The Lightning Thief* was developed into a movie. Starring Pierce Brosnan and Uma Thurman, the movie made more than $225 million. It was **nominated** for several MTV Movie and Teen Choice awards. The movie was so well received that its producers decided to continue the series. The sequel, *The Sea of Monsters*, was released in 2013. Most of the actors reprised their roles. It earned more than $200 million at the box office.

The Percy Jackson films star Logan Lerman, Alexandria Daddario and Brandon T. Jackson.

Today, Rick lives in Boston, Massachusetts with his family. He has more than enough ideas for new books he wants to write. He started a new series, called Trials of Apollo, in 2015. It is about the Greek god, Apollo, who loses his power. Apollo finds himself as a normal teenage boy in New York City. Rick's fans will be happy to hear that the new series is set in Percy Jackson's world. Rick is planning to have five books in the Trials of Apollo series.

At the same time, Rick is working on more books in the Magnus Chase series. The next book is called *The Hammer of Thor.* Teaching readers about mythology through his writing remains one of Rick's main goals. So far, he has introduced his readers to the gods of Ancient Greece, Rome, Egypt, and Scandinavia. Who knows what other myths Rick will decide to bring alive for his readers in the coming years?

Insider Info

One of Rick's favorite parts of being a children's author is meeting his fans. Thanks to them, Rick's books have become international best sellers, selling millions of copies around the world. Part of this success is thanks to Rick's relationship with his young readers.

Rick pays attention to his fans' comments on his books. He uses his readers' suggestions to create new stories and characters. When Rick's fans wanted more books about Percy Jackson, Rick listened. He created another series called Heroes of Olympus. These books brought back many of the characters from the Percy Jackson series.

Even though Rick loves interacting with his readers, he has had to reduce the number of public appearances. Attending events was taking him away from his

Some of Rick's fans come to his book signings dressed in clothes based on elements of his books.

family for long periods. His writing was suffering as well. Today, he only attends events that his publisher plans for him. Still, his calendar is very full. For example, Rick did an eight-day tour for *The Sword of Summer.* In those eight days, he was busy speaking to his fans and conducting interviews. He also signed about 10,000 books for his readers and fans.

Rick uses his website to communicate with his fans. The site contains information about Rick and his books, along with a **blog** that provides updates on what Rick is reading and writing. If Rick is going to be visiting a bookstore or appearing on television, he makes sure that his site informs his fans of the date or location of the visit.

Rick Riordan Website

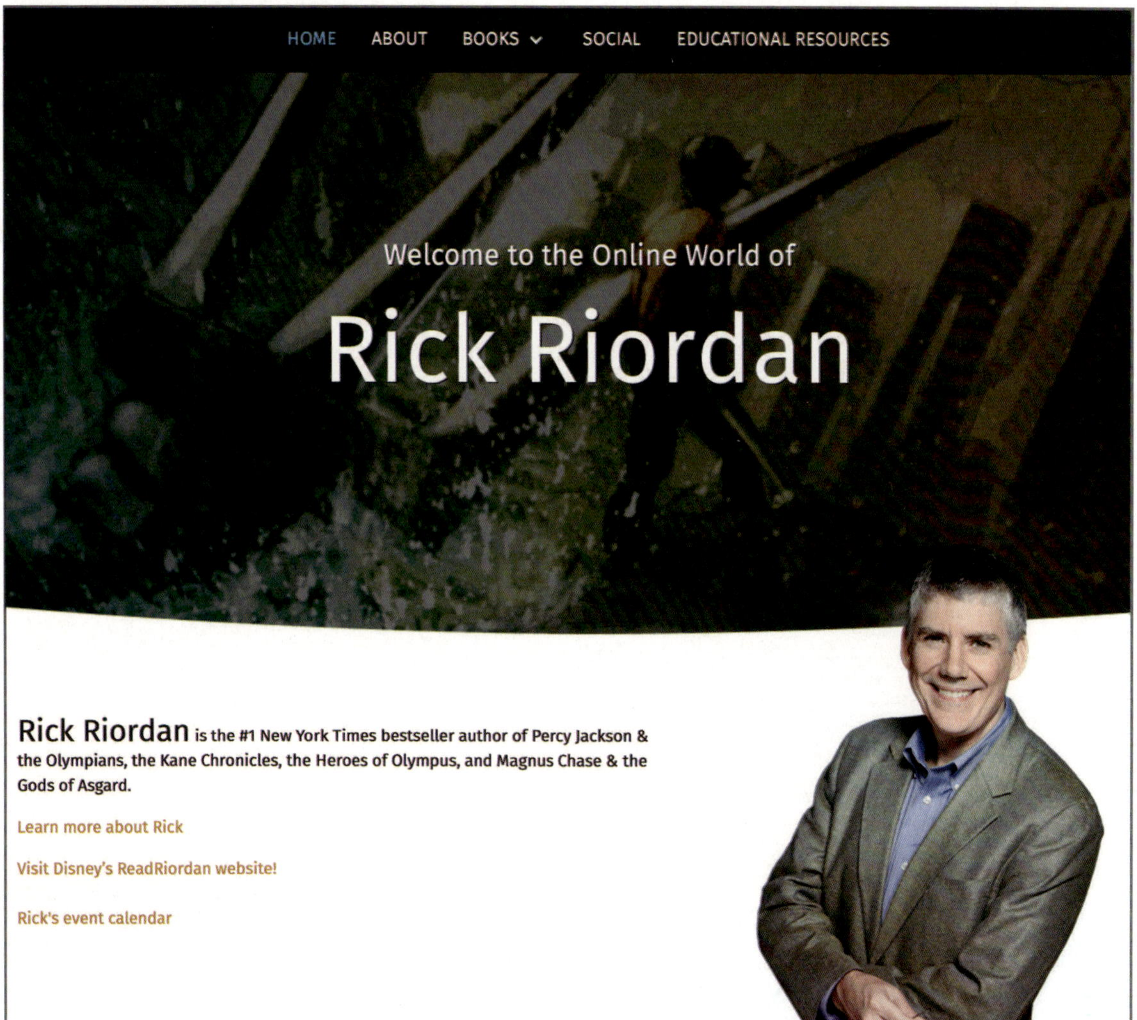

Basic Biography Writing

All of the parts of a biography work together to tell the story of a person's life. Find out how these elements combine by writing a biography. Begin by choosing a person whose story fascinates you. You will have to research the person's life by using library books and the reliable websites. You can also email the person or write him or her a letter. The person might agree to answer your questions directly.

Use a basic biography outline, such as the one below, to guide you in writing the biography. Answer each of the questions listed using the information you have gathered. Each heading on the basic biography outline will form an important part of the person's story.

Parts of a Biography

Early Life

Where and when was the person born?
What is known about the person's family and friends?
Did the person grow up in unusual circumstances?

Growing Up

Who had the most influence on the person?
Did he or she receive assistance from others?
Did the person have a positive attitude?

Developing Skills

What was the person's education?
What was the person's first job or work experience?
What obstacles did the person overcome?

Early Achievements

What was the person's most important early success?
What processes does this person use in his or her work?
Which of the person's traits were most helpful in his or her work?

Person Today

Has the person received awards or recognition for accomplishments?
What is the person's life's work?
How have the person's accomplishments served others?

Quiz

1 Where and when was Rick Riordan born?

June 5, 1964, in San Antonio, Texas

2 What eighth-grade teacher encouraged Rick to write?

His English teacher Mrs. Pabst

3 How old was Rick when he submitted his first piece of writing for publication?

12 years old

4 What did Rick first want to be when he was in college?

A musician

5 Which subjects did Rick study at the University of Texas at Austin?

English and history

6 What type of books did Rick first write and for whom?

Mystery books for adults

7 What is the name of the summer camp Percy Jackson attends?

Camp Half-Blood

8 Which person in Rick's life inspired the character of Percy Jackson?

His son, Haley

9 Rick's books are based on the mythology of which ancient civilizations?

Greece, Rome, Egypt, and Scandinavia

10 What is the name of the book series that Rick co-writes with other children's authors?

The 39 Clues

Author Speak

The field of writing has its own language. Understanding some of the more common writing terms will allow you to discuss your ideas about books.

action: the moving events of a work of fiction

antagonist: the person in the story who opposes the main character

autobiography: a history of a person's life written by that person

biography: a written account of another person's life

character: a person in a story, poem, or play

climax: the most exciting moment or turning point in a story

episode: a scene or short piece of action in a story

fiction: stories about characters and events that are not real

foreshadow: hinting at something that is going to happen later in the book

imagery: a written description of a thing or idea that brings an image to mind

narrator: the speaker of the story who relates the events

nonfiction: writing that deals with real people and events

novel: published writing of considerable length that portrays characters within a story

plot: the order of events in a work of fiction

protagonist: the leading character of a story; often a likable character

resolution: the end of the story, when the conflict is settled

scene: a single episode in a story

setting: the place and time in which a work of fiction occurs

theme: an idea that runs throughout a work of fiction

Key Words

attention deficit hyperactivity disorder: a condition in which a person is unable to pay attention to a task for a steady period of time and is easily distracted

blog: a web log that is regularly updated, often using informal language.

civilizations: social groups that have a distinctive cultural and economic organization

discipline: controlled behavior, or self-control

draft: a rough copy of a story

dyslexia: a condition that affects a person's ability to read, write, and spell

folktales: stories told orally among a group of people

genre: a category or group of art or literature

Golden Fleece: from Greek mythology, the hair of a winged ram that was stolen from the king of Colchis

graphic design: the art of using images, text, and graphic elements to communicate information

literature: writing of lasting value, including plays, poems, and novels

manuscript: a polished draft of a story before it is published

Medieval: a period of European history dating from the 5th to the 15th century

mythology: stories about supernatural creatures

nominated: entered as a candidate for an award

Norse: something Scandinavian in origin

revised: changed

sequel: a story that is related to a previous story

vocational: of or relating to an occupation or job

Index

LIGHTBOX

SUPPLEMENTARY RESOURCES

Click on the plus icon ⊕ found in the bottom left corner of each spread to open additional teacher resources.

- Download and print the book's quizzes and activities
- Access curriculum correlations
- Explore additional web applications that enhance the Lightbox experience

LIGHTBOX DIGITAL TITLES
Packed full of integrated media

VIDEOS

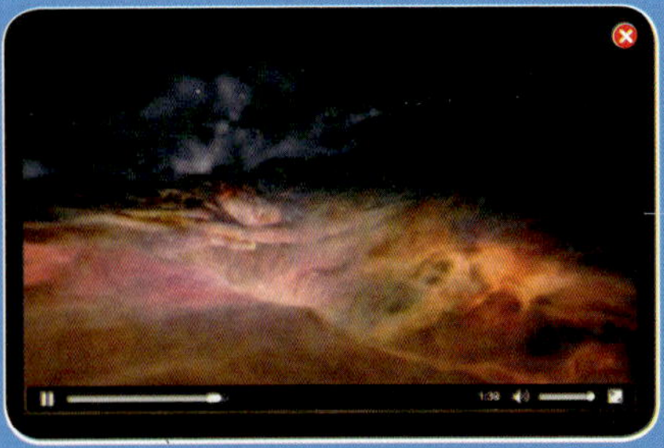

INTERACTIVE MAPS

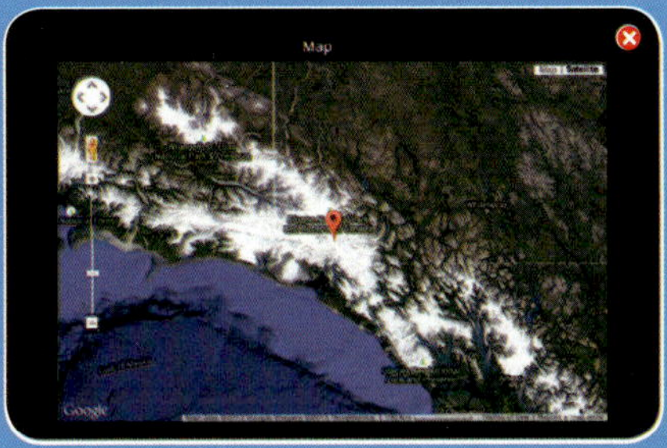

WEBLINKS

SLIDESHOWS

QUIZZES

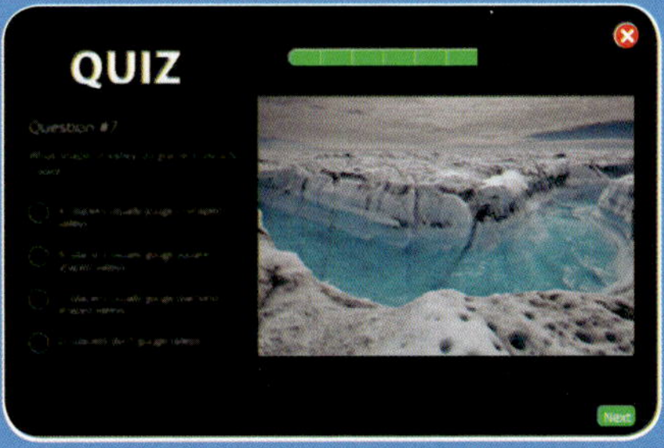

OPTIMIZED FOR

- ✓ TABLETS
- ✓ WHITEBOARDS
- ✓ COMPUTERS
- ✓ AND MUCH MORE!

Published by Smartbook Media Inc.
350 5th Avenue, 59th Floor
New York, NY 10118
Website: www.openlightbox.com

Library of Congress Control Number: 2016931414

ISBN 978-1-5105-1226-9 (hardcover)
ISBN 978-1-5105-1227-6 (multi-user eBook)

Printed in Brainerd, Minnesota, United States
1 2 3 4 5 6 7 8 9 0 20 19 18 17 16

032016
031816

Project Coordinator Jared Siemens
Designer Mandy Christiansen

Photo Credits
Every reasonable effort has been made to trace ownership and to obtain permission to reprint copyright material. The publisher would be pleased to have any errors or omissions brought to its attention so that they may be corrected in subsequent printings.

The publisher acknowledges Getty Images, Corbis Images, Alamy, Shutterstock, Newscom, and iStock as its primary image suppliers for this title.